Cool Smoothies

Fast, Fun, Frozen Treats

Cookbook Resources, LLC
Highland Village, Texas

Cool Smoothies
Fast, Fun, Frozen Treats

Printed September 2011

International Standard Book Number: 978-1-59769-042-3

Library of Congress Control Number: 2010005016

Library of Congress Cataloging-in-Publication Data

     Cool smoothies : fast, fun frozen treats.
        p. cm.
     Includes index.
     ISBN 978-1-59769-042-3
     1. Blenders (Cookery) 2. Smoothies (Beverages) I. Cookbook Resources, LLC. II. Title.

     TX840.B5C68 2010
     641.8'75--dc22

               2010005016

Cover and design by Nancy Bohanan

Edited, Designed and Published in the United States of America and Manufactured in China by
Cookbook Resources, LLC
541 Doubletree Drive
Highland Village, Texas 75077

Toll free 866-229-2665

www.cookbookresources.com

Bringing Family and Friends to the Table

Welcome to Smoothie World!

Smoothies are the very best way to get vitamins and minerals! They are the best fast foods you can make because they are so quick, easy and nutritious.

They take the place of our favorite milkshakes loaded with sugar, fat and calories. When you make creamy, slushy smoothies, you don't even realize there's no ice cream.

Throw a handful of frozen strawberries, a frozen banana, some milk or orange juice into a blender and you've got a speedy snack. Add yogurt, tofu, wheat germ, protein powder and some blueberries and you've got breakfast. Combine carrots, spinach, an orange and some silken tofu and you have lunch or dinner.

Smoothies are so easy you won't believe it. Don't worry about exact measurements or precise ingredients, just blend some of the items you have and you'll be shocked at the flavor and nutrition.

It's easy to be smart when you make healthy, nutritious smoothies. They are the other "fast food"... the best way to get your daily dose of vitamins and minerals.

Contents

Fruit Smoothies

Contents

Fruit Smoothies — continued

Vegetable Smoothies

Anatomy of Smoothies

Base:

- Fruits and vegetables
- Nuts and seeds

Liquids:

- **Creamy liquids:** low-fat yogurt, silken tofu, ice cream, sherbet, sorbet; (You need to use a thinner liquid in addition to the creamy liquids to blend well.)

- **Thinner liquids:** low-fat milk, low-fat soy milk, fruit juices, vegetable juices, water, green tea, coffee, chai

Additions (optional):

- **Flavor additions:** dates, raisins, fruit juice concentrates, peanut butter, honey, maple syrup, stevia

- **Thickening additions:** cashews, almonds, avocado, peanut butter

- **Nutritional additions:** wheat germ, flaxseed oil, spirulina (kelp, seaweed), bee pollen, cacao, pumpkin seeds, sunflower seeds, acerola powder, whey protein powder, protein drinks, ginseng, vitamin C powder, echinea, lechitin, carob

Definitions:

- **Bee Pollen:** Bee pollen is the powdery substance produced by flowers and gathered by bees. It is very nutritious and contains vitamin C, B-complex vitamins and amino acids.

- **Calcium:** Calcium is an essential mineral for bone and teeth health. It also helps the functioning of muscles and nerves.

  A calcium deficiency has no overt symptoms until they become acute and manifest in renal failure, lethargy, convulsions and abnormal heart rhythms.

- **Echinea:** Echinea has anti-inflammatory properties and antibiotic properties which makes it good for colds, energy, blood pressure.

- **Lechitin:** Lechitin aids brain function, cell growth and energy.

- **Magnesium:** Magnesium is an essential mineral for bones and cells in tissues, organs and blood. It helps to maintain a steady heart rhythm, muscle and nerve function, normal blood pressure and stable blood sugar levels.

  A magnesium deficiency may result in migraines, sensitivity to light and sound, trembling, insomnia, allergies and muscle weakness.

Continued next page...

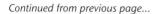

Continued from previous page...

- **Organic:** Organic fruits and vegetables are grown without pesticides or chemical fertilizers. The vitamin and mineral content of fruits and vegetables are usually higher than commercially grown ones.

- **Phosphorus:** Phosphorus is a major component of bone structure and helps blood maintain oxygen levels sufficient to supply tissues in the body.

  A lack of phosphorus may show up as bone pain, loss of appetite, tingling in extremities or muscle weakness.

- **Potassium:** Potassium is essential to the body's health, growth and systems. It is an electrolyte which balances water between cells and the body's fluids. It affects the contraction of muscles, stimulation of nerves and heart function.

  A potassium deficiency may exhibit as fatigue, cramps, muscle weakness or abnormal heart rhythm.

- **Soy milk:** Natural soy milk is a non-dairy liquid created when liquid is pressed out of soybeans. It has no chemicals, additives or preservatives. It is a good source of proteins, isoflavones and B-vitamins and is lactose free.

Continued next page...

Continued from previous page...

- **Stevia:** Stevia is a natural sweetener and sugar substitute. It has no calories and is sweeter than honey.

- **Tofu:** Tofu is the semi-solid part of milk after it separates from the liquid part called whey. It is loaded with protein, has no cholesterol and boosts the immune system. There are two forms of tofu: soft and firm. Soft or silken tofu is a little sweeter and is used for smoothies.

- **Wheat germ:** Wheat germ is a health food basic and nutritional additive with iron, zinc and fiber. It comes from the wheat kernel. It reduces the risk of heart disease, osteoporosis and dementia.

- **Whey protein:** Whey protein is produced when milk is made into cheese. It is a valuable source of protein.

- **Yogurt:** Yogurt is a fermented dairy product made by adding bacterial cultures to milk which changes sugar in cow's milk to lactic acid. It is good for digestive tract, lowers LDL (bad) cholesterol, raises HDL (good) cholesterol and is an excellent source of vitamins and minerals.

Check Your Vitamins

VITAMINS	BENEFITS	FRUITS	VEGETABLES	NUTS/SEEDS
Vitamin A	Immunity Cell growth Vision Bone growth Teeth health Healthy skin and hair	Blackberries Cantaloupes Kiwifruit Peaches Tomatoes Watermelon	Asparagus Avocado Broccoli Carrots Green bell pepper Kale Squash, yellow Sweet potato	Almonds Pecans Pine nuts Pistachios Pumpkin seeds Sunflower seeds
Vitamin B1 (Thiamine)	Energy Heart Muscles	Watermelon	Avocado Peas	None
Vitamin B2 (Riboflavin)	Red blood cells Energy	Kiwifruit	Avocado	None
Vitamin B3 (Niacin)	Digestive system Healthy skin Converts food to energy	Bananas Cantaloupe Peaches Tomatoes Watermelon	Asparagus Avocado Broccoli Carrots Kale Potatoes Squash	Almonds Peanuts Pine nuts
Vitamin B5 (Pantothenic acid)	Metabolism Good cholesterol	Bananas Oranges	Avocado Broccoli Carrots Cauliflower Corn Potatoes	None
Vitamin B6 (Pyridoxine)	Red blood cells Dissemination of proteins	Bananas Watermelon	Avocado Carrots Potatoes	None
Vitamin B9 (Folate)	Red blood cells Brain functions Pregnancy	Bananas Blackberries Cantaloupe Oranges Strawberries Tomatoes	Asparagus Avocado Broccoli Carrots Corn Kale Onions Potatoes	Almonds Cashews Peanuts Pecans Pine nuts Pistachios Walnuts

Check Your Vitamins

VITAMINS	BENEFITS	FRUITS	VEGETABLES	NUTS/SEEDS
Vitamin B12	Red blood cells Central nervous system (only available in fish, meat, dairy)	None	None	None
Vitamin C	Supplies antioxidants	Apples Bananas Blackberries Cantaloupe Grapes Oranges Peaches Tomatoes Watermelon	Asparagus Avocado Broccoli Carrots Cauliflower Cucumber Green bell peppers Kale Onions Potatoes Spinach Squash	None
Vitamin D (Sunshine vitamin)	Helps body absorb calcium and magnesium Healthy teeth Healthy bones	None	Mushrooms	None
Vitamin E	Supplies antioxidants Red blood cells Wrinkle resistance Heals skin	Apples Bananas Blackberries Kiwifruit	None	Almonds Peanuts Pine nuts Sunflower Seeds
Vitamin K	Bone health Blood clotting	None	Broccoli Kale Spinach All dark greens	Cashews Pine nuts

Basic Smoothie

Base:

1 cup fresh or frozen fruit(s) and/or vegetable(s)

Liquid:

1 cup liquid (milk, soy milk, juices, almond milk,
        coffee, tea, coconut milk, water)

Blend all ingredients. Makes 1 smoothie.

*TIP: The thickness of smoothies will vary
        depending on the type of fruits/vegetables
        used and whether you use fresh or frozen
        fruits/vegetables.*

*If your smoothie is too runny, you can either
add more of your base (fruits or vegetables)
or a thickening addition. If your smoothie is
too thick, just add more liquid.*

*Blenders were invented by Stephen
Poplawski when in 1922 he became
the first person to put a spinning
blade at the bottom of a small
electric appliance to make
Horlick's malted milkshakes.*

Additions to Basic Smoothie:

- **Thickening Additions:** yogurt, silken tofu, avocado, canned pumpkin, non-fat powdered milk, ice cream, frozen yogurt, sorbet, sherbet, ice

- **Flavor Additions:** honey, stevia natural sweetener, flavor extracts, cocoa powder, peanut butter

- **Healthy Additions:** protein powder, wheat germ, flaxseed, seeds, nuts

Basic Smoothie Tips

- For cold, thicker smoothies, use slightly frozen fruits or vegetables. Lay slices of fruit on baking pan, freeze and store in plastic bags. Freeze fruit juices in ice cube trays. Large pieces of frozen fruit need to thaw a little before blending.

- For thinner smoothies, use fresh fruits and vegetables and more liquid.

- The average amount of liquid for smoothies is about 1 cup. If you like thick, slushy smoothies, only use enough liquid to blend the ingredients. If you like thinner smoothies, add a little more liquid.

- Put the liquid in the blender first. Fruits and vegetables will blend better. You may have to stir the mixture several times after you start the blender.

Continued next page...

Continued from previous page...

- Replace a banana with an avocado to cut down on sugar. Bananas and avocados give smoothies a creamy texture. Avocados are loaded with potassium, B-complex vitamin, fiber and antioxidants. They are high in oleic acids which reduce bad LDL cholesterol and increase good HDL healthy cholesterol.

- Use organic fruits and vegetables because they don't have wax on the outside and haven't been exposed to agricultural chemicals. It's always best to use organic greens because they haven't been exposed to pesticides.

- Blend greens and vegetables with sweeter fruits to balance the flavor of vegetables. The best blend is about 60% fruits and 40% vegetables. Most of the time the flavors   of fruits overpower the flavor of vegetables.

- Peanut butter is a good addition to smoothies because it is full of nutrients and fiber and it will help you feel fuller longer.

- For a creamier smoothie, place banana in plastic wrap and freeze for about 1 hour before making the smoothie.

Fruit Smoothies

Banana Silk

1 cup low-fat milk or soy milk
1 cup silken tofu
2 large ripe bananas, peeled,
   sliced
¼ cup honey, optional
¼ cup slivered almonds, optional

Combine all ingredients in blender with ½ cup crushed ice and process until smooth. Serve immediately. Makes 2 smoothies.

TIP: *For a creamier smoothie, place banana in plastic wrap and freeze for about 1 hour before making the smoothie.*

Why are bananas never lonely?

Because they hang around in bunches!

Peanut Butter-Banana Dana

1 cup low-fat milk or soy milk
2 bananas, peeled, sliced
¼ cup peanut butter

Combine all ingredients in blender and blend until smooth.

Add ½ to 1 cup ice cubes and blend until smooth. Makes 1 to 2 smoothies.

Americans eat more than 700 million pounds of peanut butter per year. It takes about 850 peanuts to make an 18-ounce jar of peanut butter.

A) How many 18-ounce jars of peanut butter are in 700 million pounds?

B) How many peanuts are used to make 700 million pounds of peanut butter?

A) 622,222,222 18-ounce jars
B) 528,888,888,700 peanuts

Banana-Cocoa Smoothie

1 cup low-fat soy milk
½ cup silken vanilla tofu
1 banana, peeled, sliced
2 tablespoons cocoa powder
1 tablespoon honey

Place all ingredients in blender
with ½ to 1 cup ice cubes and
process until creamy. Makes
1 smoothie.

Why did the banana go out with
a prune?

Because he couldn't get a date!

22

Bananalicious

1 cup low-fat milk
¼ cup frozen orange juice
     concentrate
1 banana, peeled, sliced
1 packet instant breakfast drink
1 tablespoon honey

Place all ingredients in
blender with several ice cubes
and process until desired
consistency. Makes 1 smoothie.

*The average American consumes
about 30 pounds of bananas a
year. Bananas are full of vitamin C,
potassium and dietary fiber.*

Good Morning Sunshine

2 cups low-fat milk or low-fat
      vanilla yogurt
2 bananas, peeled, sliced
1 cup fresh pineapple chunks
4 - 6 Clementine oranges,
      peeled

Add all ingredients to blender
and process until smooth and
creamy. Makes 2 smoothies.

TIP: Delicious served over ice.

*A pineapple can grow to weigh
more than 20 pounds!*

Sittin' by the Dock on the Bay

1½ cups pineapple juice or
    orange juice, chilled
1 (6 ounce) carton low-fat
    vanilla yogurt
1 banana, peeled, sliced
1 mango, peeled, sliced

Process banana slices, mango,
juice and yogurt in blender until
smooth. Scrape sides of blender
and mix. Serve immediately.
Makes 1 smoothie.

*TIP: For a creamier smoothie, place fruit in
    plastic wrap and freeze for about
    1 hour before making the smoothie.*

Tofu-Honey

*Here's a healthy treat
for smoothie lovers.*

1 cup low-fat milk or soy milk
1 cup silken tofu
2 medium bananas, peeled,
    sliced
2 - 3 tablespoons honey
1 teaspoon almond extract or
    vanilla

Combine all ingredients and
½ cup crushed ice in blender
and process until smooth.
Makes 2 smoothies.

*Next time you purchase grapes, place
a few clusters in the freezer. When
you need a lift, the frozen grapes will
pick you right up!*

Soy Good For You

1 cup low-fat soy milk
1 cup silken tofu
1 banana, peeled, sliced
1½ cups frozen blueberries

Place all ingredients in blender with several ice cubes and process until creamy. Makes 1 to 2 smoothies.

How do basketball players stay cool?

They sit next to their fans.

Berry Mix-Up

1 cup orange juice
1 cup silken tofu
1 (6 ounce) carton low-fat
    blueberry yogurt
1½ cups frozen mixed berries

Place all ingredients in blender
with several ice cubes and
process until creamy. Makes
2 smoothies.

Smoothies are especially smart
for kids because they can get
their vitamins and minerals without
thinking about it. The flavors
of fruits cover up the flavor of
vegetables like broccoli and greens
that they may not normally eat.

Healthy Happy Sipper

1 cup raspberry-cranberry
    juice, chilled
½ cup silken tofu
1 banana, peeled, sliced
¾ cup frozen mixed berries
1 tablespoon flaxseed, optional

Pour all ingredients in blender
and process until smooth. Makes
1 smoothie.

What did Snow White say when
her photographs were ready?

"I knew one day my prints would
come."

Berry Blessing

¾ cup orange juice
1 (6 ounce) carton low-fat
    vanilla yogurt
1½ cups fresh berries
¼ cup nonfat dry milk
1 tablespoon wheat germ,
    optional
1 tablespoon honey
½ teaspoon vanilla extract

Place all ingredients in blender
with several ice cubes and
process until creamy. Makes
1 smoothie.

Honey is the only food for humans
that never spoils. It is edible even
after 1,000 years.

Easy, Breezy Strawberry Smoothie

- 1 cup low-fat milk or soy milk
- 1 (6 ounce) carton vanilla yogurt
- 1 banana
- 1 cup frozen blueberries
- 1 cup sliced fresh or frozen strawberries

Combine all ingredients in blender. Process until smooth. Makes 2 smoothies.

TIP: Use low-fat milk, yogurt, soy milk and tofu instead of whole milk, etc. There is no difference in the taste and flavor of smoothies.

I would rather try to carry 10 plastic grocery bags in each hand than make two trips to bring in my groceries.

Rise and Shine

2½ cups low-fat milk
2 bananas, peeled, sliced
½ cup frozen blueberries
½ cup frozen unsweetened
      strawberries
2 teaspoons peanut butter
1 tablespoon honey

Place all ingredients into blender
and process until smooth. Serve
immediately. Makes 2 smoothies.

*A smoothie or milkshake loaded
with ice cream, sweet syrups and
other high sugar, high fat ingredients
can have up to 1,000 calories.*

*Did you know seaweed is used to
thicken ice cream?*

Sweet and Dandy

- 1 cup unsweetened cranberry juice
- 1 cup frozen mixed berries
- 1 banana, peeled, sliced
- 1 tablespoon wheat germ, optional
- 1 tablespoon flaxseed oil, optional
- 2 teaspoons lemon juice
- ⅛ teaspoon stevia or sweetener

Place all ingredients in blender with several ice cubes; process until creamy. Makes 1 smoothie.

TIP: Use more cranberry juice for a thinner smoothie.

By Golly, Wow!

1 cup low-fat milk
1 (6 ounce) carton vanilla low-fat yogurt
1 cup canned apricot halves with juice
1 cup frozen unsweetened strawberries

Place all ingredients in blender with several ice cubes and process until creamy. Makes 1 smoothie

Time may be a great healer, but it's a lousy beautician.

Bright-and-Early Smoothie

1¼ cups orange juice
½ cup low-fat silken tofu or low-
    fat vanilla yogurt
1¼ cups frozen mixed berries
1 banana, peeled, sliced
1 tablespoon stevia or
    sweetener

Place all ingredients in blender
with several ice cubes and
process until creamy. Makes
2 smoothies.

*TIP: For a little variety, experiment with
    different flavors of low-fat yogurt.*

Knock, Knock.   Who's there?

Banana.   Banana who?

Banana split so ice creamed!

Sweet Sensation

1 cup orange juice, chilled
1 ripe banana, peeled, sliced
1 ripe peach, peeled, cubed
1 cup blueberries

Put orange juice in blender.
Add banana, peach, blueberries
and 1 cup ice cubes.

Blend on high speed until slushy.
Makes 1 to 2 smoothies.

*TIP: For a creamier smoothie, place fruit in
plastic wrap and freeze for about
1 hour before making the smoothie.*

*There is a great need for a sarcasm
font in e-mail.*

Blueberry-Banana Power

1 cup low-fat milk
1 banana, peeled, sliced
1 cup frozen blueberries

Place all ingredients in blender
with several ice cubes and
process until creamy. Makes
1 smoothie.

Blueberries are considered a "super food" because researchers are finding more and more health benefits for humans. Blueberries help prevent cancer, lessen the effects of aging, and lower cholesterol to work against heart disease.

Blueberry Bomb

1 cup cranberry juice cocktail,
    chilled
1 (6 ounce) carton low-fat
    blueberry yogurt
1 cup frozen blueberries

Place all ingredients in blender
with several ice cubes and
process until creamy. Makes
1 smoothie.

*TIP: You can process just the ingredients
and serve over ice.*

Cranberries are loaded with vitamin
C and antioxidants that help
cleanse the body. They help to
keep bacteria from sticking inside
the body and to strengthen the
immune system.

Strawberry-Banana Dandy

1 cup orange juice
1 (6 ounce) carton low-fat
    strawberry yogurt
1 pint fresh strawberries,
    quartered
2 medium bananas, peeled,
    sliced

Place all ingredients in blender
and process until smooth.

Serve as is or over crushed ice.
Makes 2 smoothies.

Bananas are added to smoothies for sweetness, nutrition and texture. Avocados do the same thing and are great substitutes for bananas because they have less sugar and more good HDL cholesterol.

Berry Merry Berries

1 cup apple juice, chilled
¼ cup silken tofu
1 cup frozen mixed berries
½ banana, peeled, sliced

Combine all ingredients in blender with ½ cup ice; process until smooth. Makes 1 smoothie.

Tofu is made from soybeans, water and a coagulant. By itself it is almost tasteless, but absorbs the flavors of other ingredients. It is high in protein and calcium and is a staple for vegetarians.

Cranberries, blueberries and Concord grapes are the only major fruits native to North America.

Cool Reggae Fruit Smoothie

1 cup low-fat milk
2 (6 ounce) cartons low-fat
    vanilla yogurt
1 cup frozen blueberries
1 cup frozen peach slices
1 (8 ounce) can pineapple
    chunks, drained

Process all ingredients in
blender until smooth. (If drink is
not sweet enough, add sugar or
sweetener.) Makes 2 smoothies.

Christopher Columbus found
pineapples on the Caribbean island
of Guadeloupe in 1493 and took
them back to Spain. The Spanish
used the word for pine cone
("piña") for them because they
resembled pine cones.

Simple Simon's Simple Smoothie

1 cup limeade
1 (6 ounce) carton low-fat key
    lime yogurt
1 banana, peeled, sliced

Place all ingredients in blender with 1 to 2 cups ice and process until desired consistency. Makes 1 smoothie.

TIP: For a creamier smoothie, place banana in plastic wrap and freeze for about 1 hour before making the smoothie.

Raising teenagers is like trying to nail jelly to a tree.

Kiwi Mate

1 cup orange juice
2 kiwifruit, peeled, sliced
2 apples, cored, quartered
½ lime, halved

Place all ingredients, except lime, in blender with several ice cubes. Squeeze juice from lime, add to blender and process until creamy. Makes 1 smoothie.

Kiwifruit (or kiwi) were first called Chinese gooseberries. During the 1950's New Zealand changed the name to "kiwi", the nickname of New Zealand people.

Cherry-Chocolate Dessert

⅔ cup low-fat milk or vanilla
    soy milk
½ cup cranberry-raspberry
    juice, chilled
1 (6 ounce) carton low-fat
    chocolate yogurt
2 cups unsweetened frozen
    pitted cherries
2 tablespoons Nutella®

Add all ingredients to blender
and process until creamy.
Add ice if desired. Makes
2 smoothies.

*TIP: Nutella® is a hazelnut spread you can
    find in the grocery store next to the
    peanut butter.*

What kind of apple isn't an apple?

A crab apple.

Cherry Pit Spitter

1 cup low-fat vanilla soy milk
1 (6 ounce) carton low-fat
     vanilla yogurt
2 cups pitted, frozen cherries

Place all ingredients in blender
with several ice cubes and
process until creamy. Makes
1 to 2 smoothies.

The Guinness Book of World Records
recognizes Michigan's Cherry Pit
Spit as an official competition. It
registered the world record of 95 feet
9 inches for a spit pit.

When a spiffy cherry pit spitter
spit pits in the spring, the pits went
splish-splash. When the cherry pit
spitter ran out of pits to spit, he
spat the pits he split.

The Mango Tango

1 cup orange juice, chilled
1 cup pineapple juice, chilled
1½ cups frozen mango slices
1 small banana, peeled, sliced

Pour all ingredients into blender
and process until smooth.
Serve as is or over ice. Makes
2 smoothies.

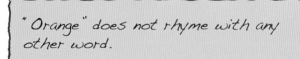

*"Orange" does not rhyme with any
other word.*

Monkey Mango Smoothie

1 cup low-fat milk
1 cup frozen cubed mango
1 ripe banana, peeled, sliced
1 teaspoon honey
¼ teaspoon vanilla extract

Combine all ingredients in blender. Process until smooth. Makes 1 smoothie.

Most fruits have high water content and can easily be juiced, but avocados, mangoes, bananas, papayas need juice or milk with them.

Tropical Lassi

1 cup orange juice
1 (6 ounce) carton low-fat
   vanilla yogurt
1 cup peeled, sliced mango
⅓ cup peach sorbet

Place all ingredients in blender
with several ice cubes and
process until creamy. Makes
1 smoothie.

*Lassi is a traditional Indian drink
that is made by blending milk,
yogurt and sometimes fruits.*

*A ripe watermelon sounds hollow
when thumped. Look for a slightly
yellowish color on the underside.*

Honeydew This

1 cup white grape juice, chilled
1 tablespoon lime juice
⅓ cup lemon sorbet
1 cup honeydew melon chunks
2 kiwifruit, peeled, quartered
1 banana, peeled, sliced

Place all ingredients in blender with several ice cubes and process until creamy. Makes 1 smoothie.

Eating a good breakfast of healthy smoothies, cereals and breakfast drinks provides the best fuel for cognitive performance, more energy, more alertness and better memory; and helps kids maintain the best weight.

Orange Sunrise

1 cup low-fat milk or soy milk
1 (6 ounce) carton low-fat
    orange yogurt
1 large orange, peeled,
    quartered
1 teaspoon vanilla extract

Pour all ingredients plus ½ cup ice cubes into blender and process until smooth. Serve immediately. Makes 1 smoothie.

Families are like fudge... mostly sweet with a few nuts!

Orange Creamsicle

½ cup low-fat milk or soy milk
1 (6 ounce) carton low-fat
    vanilla yogurt
1 (11 ounce) can mandarin
    oranges with juice
½ cup pineapple chunks
1 - 2 tablespoons honey

Lay oranges and pineapple chunks on baking sheet and freeze for about 1 hour.

Place all ingredients in blender and process until smooth. Makes 2 smoothies.

Honey is sometimes used for antifreeze mixtures and in the center of golf balls.

Montego Bay Smoothie

1 cup low-fat milk or soy milk
1 (6 ounce) carton low-fat
      coconut-cream pie yogurt
1½ heaping cups papaya,
      peeled, seeded, cubed
1½ heaping cups ripe melon,
      cubed
1 very ripe large banana,
      peeled, sliced

Place all ingredients in blender
and puree until smooth. Pour into
glasses and serve immediately.
Makes 2 smoothies.

*Low-fat milk, yogurt and soy milk
are used in smoothies because
they have no effect on flavor.*

Orange Crush Smoothie

This is a great, nutritious snack.

1 cup light vanilla soy milk
1 (6 ounce) carton low-fat
    vanilla yogurt
½ cup frozen orange juice
    concentrate, thawed
1 orange, peeled, quartered

Process all ingredients until smooth. Makes 1 smoothie.

*TIP: Try different frozen fruit juice
     concentrates to make your own
     favorite concoction.*

*Oranges are one of the most
popular fruits in the world. They
are excellent sources for vitamin C
and are high in dietary fiber, folate,
vitamin B₁, potassium and calcium.*

*The juiciest oranges are firm and
heavy for their size.*

Double Peach Cream

1 cup peach nectar, chilled
1 (6 ounce) carton low-fat
      peach yogurt
1 cup frozen sliced peaches

Place peach slices in plastic wrap and freeze about 1 hour.

Place all ingredients in blender with several ice cubes and process until creamy. Makes 1 to 2 smoothies.

" In general, mankind, since the improvement in cookery, eats twice as much as nature requires."
                    Benjamin Franklin

Peach Oink

1 cup low-fat milk
1 tablespoon fresh lemon juice
1 cup vanilla ice cream
2 cups frozen sliced peaches
1 fresh peach, sliced

Place all ingredients in blender except the fresh peach. Blend until smooth. Pour in glasses.

Chop remaining peach and stir into smoothie. Serve immediately. Makes 2 smoothies.

TIP: Use several slices from fresh peach as garnish.

The tradition of giving a friend a peach started the saying, "You're a real peach."

Orange You Lucky

1½ cups vanilla soy milk
½ cup orange juice
        concentrate, thawed
4 scoops vanilla ice cream

Place all ingredients in blender
and process until creamy. Makes
2 smoothies.

Creamy Peach Dream

1 cup orange juice, chilled
3 - 4 scoops vanilla ice cream
1 cup fresh peeled, pitted,
        chopped peaches

Combine all ingredients in
blender and process until
smooth and creamy. Makes
2 smoothies.

Peach Groove

2 cups peach nectar, chilled
1 (6 ounce) carton low-fat
    peach yogurt
1 (6 ounce) carton low-fat
    vanilla yogurt
2 cups frozen peach slices
½ banana, peeled, sliced

Process all ingredients in blender until smooth. Makes 2 smoothies.

Peaches are native only to China. They are one of the oldest cultivated fruits in history. Some Chinese peaches are shaped like hockey pucks.

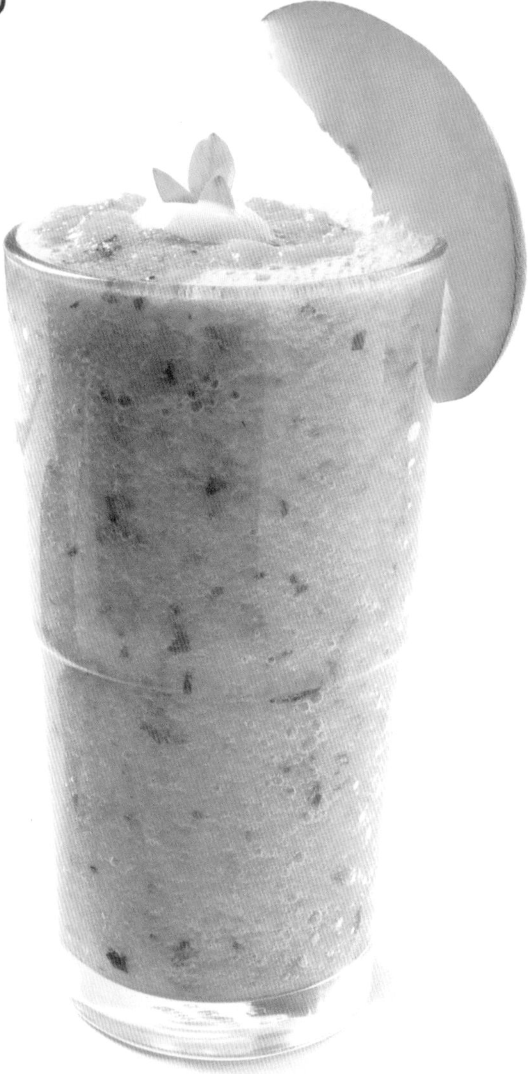

A Healthy Germy Beverage

1 cup orange juice
2 (6 ounce) cartons low-fat
    vanilla yogurt
2 bananas, peeled, sliced
2 peaches, peeled, sliced
¼ cup wheat germ, optional

Place all ingredients in blender
with about ½ cup ice cubes and
process until creamy. Makes
2 smoothies.

Wheat germ is a powerhouse
ingredient. It's loaded with folic
acid which reduces homocysteine
in the body which lessens the risk
of heart disease, osteoporosis
and dementia. It's also full of
antioxidants and fiber.

84

Hawaiian Holiday

½ cup guava nectar, chilled
1 cup canned pineapple chunks
      with juice
½ cup papaya slices
1 tablespoon lime juice
1 teaspoon grenadine

Place all ingredients in blender
with several ice cubes and
process until creamy. Makes
1 smoothie.

A small papaya contains about
300% of the recommended daily
amount of Vitamin C.

Pineapple To Go

1 cup pineapple-orange juice
¼ cup low-fat vanilla yogurt
1 cup frozen pineapple chunks

Pour all ingredients into
blender. Blend well and serve
immediately. Makes 1 smoothie.

Use unsweetened frozen fruits
instead of fruits in sweetened
syrups.

1 cup sweetened strawberries with
    syrup = 230 calories

1 cup unsweetened strawberries
    = 50 calories

Angels' Fruit Smoothie

1 cup low-fat milk or soy milk
2 (6 ounce) cartons low-fat
     vanilla yogurt
1 (8 ounce) can pineapple
     chunks with juice
1 cup frozen blueberries
1 cup frozen peach slices

Process all ingredients in
blender until smooth. Scrape
sides once or twice. Serve
immediately. Makes 2 smoothies.

" Brain freeze" was invented in 1994
by 7-Eleven to explain the pain
one feels when drinking a Slurpee
too fast. The medical term is
sphenopalatine ganglioneuralgia.

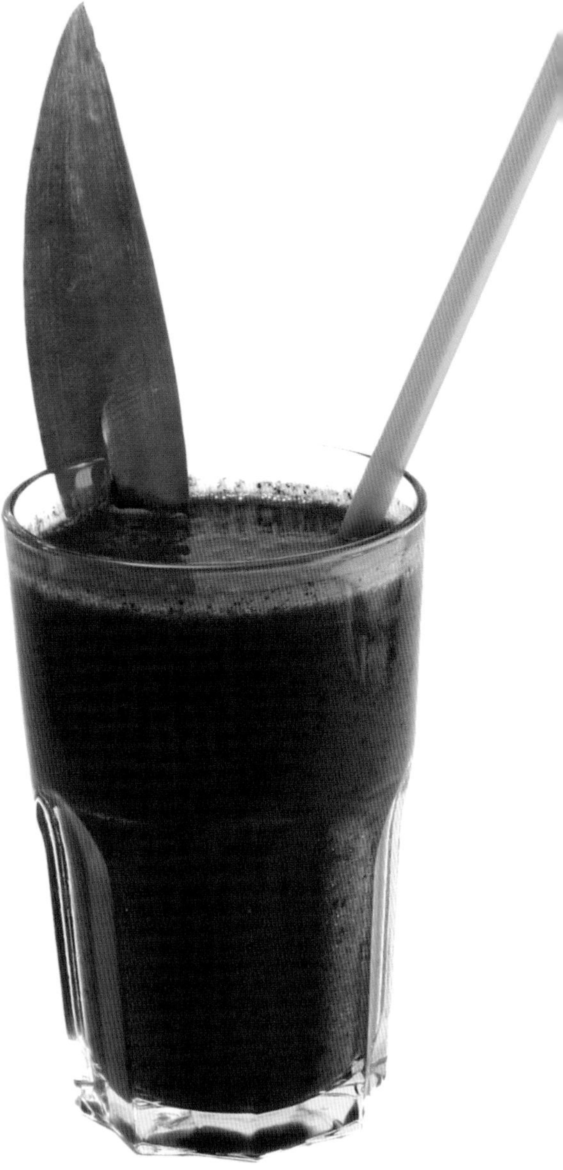

Pomegranate-Berry Blend

1 cup pomegranate juice, chilled
1 (6 ounce) carton low-fat
      yogurt
1½ cup frozen mixed berries

Place all ingredients in blender
with several ice cubes and
process until creamy. Makes
1 smoothie.

Pomegranates are super foods
because they contain lots of
calcium, potassium, iron and
phytonutrients. They help protect
the body from heart disease,
diabetes and cancer and slow down
aging. Red seeds inside the outer red
skin are edible and good for juicing.

Raspberry Delight

2 cups apple juice, chilled
1 cup frozen raspberries and
    strawberries
1 large banana, sliced
1 cup raspberry sherbet

Combine apple juice, strawberries, raspberries and banana and process for 10 to 20 seconds.

Add raspberry sherbet and process until they blend. Serve immediately. Makes 2 smoothies.

Berries are one of nature's best pleasures. They are easy and fun to eat, loaded with vitamin C, calcium, magnesium, folate and potassium and are low in calories.

Raspberry-Avocado Slush

½ cup cranberry-raspberry
    juice, chilled
½ cup orange juice, chilled
1 large avocado, peeled, pitted
1 cup frozen raspberries

Place all ingredients in blender
with several ice cubes and
process until creamy. Makes
1 smoothie.

*Believe it or not, avocados are
fruits, not vegetables. One avocado
contains more than 20 vitamins and
minerals needed for a healthy diet.
They have polyunsaturated fat
(the "good" fat), but they have
no cholesterol.*

Strawberry Icey

1 cup orange juice
1 cup frozen strawberries
1 teaspoon lemon juice
1 packet stevia or sweetener

Place all ingredients in blender
with several ice cubes and
½ cup ice water and process
until creamy. Makes 1 smoothie.

The strawberry is one of the most
popular fruits in the world. Wash
them and pat dry right before eating
so they won't absorb water.

Whey Cool

1½ cups strawberry-banana
      juice
1 (6 ounce) carton low-fat
      strawberry yogurt
1 banana, peeled, sliced
½ cup Grape-Nuts® cereal
1 scoop whey protein

Place all ingredients in blender
with several ice cubes and
process until creamy. Makes
1 smoothie.

*TIP: Sprinkle Grape Nuts® on top of
      smoothie for extra crunch.*

*Middle age is when you choose
your cereal for the fiber, not
the toy!*

Merry Berry Strawberry Smoothie

2 cups orange juice, chilled
1 (6 ounce) carton low-fat
     strawberry yogurt
1 (16 ounce) bag frozen
     strawberries
2 medium bananas, peeled,
     sliced

Place all ingredients in blender.
Process until smooth.

Serve as is or over crushed ice.
Makes 3 to 4 smoothies.

What do you call two banana peels?
A pair of slippers!

Raspberry-Cranberry Cocktail

1 cup cranberry juice cocktail,
    chilled
1 (6 ounce) carton low-fat
    strawberry yogurt
1 cup frozen unsweetened
    raspberries

Place all ingredients in blender
with several ice cubes and
process until creamy. Makes
1 smoothie.

Raw fruits and vegetables have
more vitamins and minerals than
cooked ones.

Watermelon Frost

1 cup pineapple juice, chilled
2 scoops orange sherbet
2 cups seedless watermelon
    chunks
1 cup frozen unsweetened
    strawberries

Place all ingredients in blender and process until creamy. Makes 1 to 2 smoothies.

Smoothies replace milkshakes which have lots of fats and calories to provide a healthy, refreshing drink that contains vitamins and minerals.

Summertime Watermelon Smoothie

2 cups cubed, seeded
   watermelon
2 tablespoons honey
Dash of cinnamon
1 (6 ounce) carton low-fat lemon
   yogurt

Process watermelon, honey and cinnamon just a little to mix.

Add lemon yogurt, pulse quickly and serve immediately. Makes 1 smoothie.

In Japan, they grow square watermelons so they can be stored in small spaces and fit in the refrigerator better.

Choco-Berry Zest

1 cup cranberry juice, chilled
1 (6 ounce) carton low-fat
        chocolate yogurt
1½ cups frozen unsweetened
        strawberries
1 tablespoon powdered sugar
¼ cup mini-chocolate chips

Place all ingredients in blender
except chocolate chips. Process
until smooth. Add chocolate
chips and pulse several times.
Makes 2 to 3 smoothies.

*TIP: For an extra dose of chocolate,
sprinkle mini-chocolate chips on top
of smoothie.*

*Hershey's Kisses® are named that
because the machine that makes
them looks like it is kissing the
conveyor belt.*

Popsicle Breakfast

½ cup low-fat milk
½ cup orange juice
1 (6 ounce) carton low-fat
        vanilla yogurt
1 all-fruit flavored popsicle
1 banana, peeled, sliced
⅓ cup instant oatmeal

Remove popsicle from stick
and place in blender. Add
remaining ingredients to blender
with several ice cubes and
process until smooth. Makes 1 to
2 smoothies.

"I'm a great believer in luck, and
I find the harder I work, the more
I have of it."   Thomas Jefferson

Ruby Red-Strawberry-Mango Smoothie

2 - 3 grapefruit
1 cup peeled, chopped, ripe
     mango
1 medium banana, peeled,
     sliced
1 (6 ounce) carton low-fat
     strawberry-banana yogurt
2 tablespoons honey
½ teaspoon vanilla

Slice grapefruit into halves and squeeze enough fresh juice to equal 1 cup. (Add canned grapefruit juice or orange juice if needed.)

Continued next page...

Continued from previous page...

Pour juice into blender and add mango, banana, strawberry yogurt, honey, vanilla and about ½ cup ice.

Blend for about 10 to 20 seconds or until desired consistency. Add another ½ cup ice and process until smooth. Makes 2 smoothies.

Fresh grapefruit is available year-round. From January to August, grapefruit comes primarily from California and Arizona. From October to June it comes primarily from Texas and Florida.

Tutti-Frutti Smoothie

1 cup orange juice, chilled
1 ripe banana, peeled, sliced
1 ripe peach, cut into chunks
1 cup frozen strawberries

Pour orange juice into blender
and add banana, peach,
strawberries and 1 cup ice
cubes.

Blend on high speed until
creamy. Makes 2 smoothies.

*Vitamin C is one of our most
important antioxidants. Foods
with a lot of vitamin C include
strawberries, papaya, oranges,
parsley and spinach.*

Funky Kingston Town

1 cup low-fat milk or soy milk
1 (6 ounce) carton low-fat
    vanilla yogurt
2 mangos, peeled, chopped
1 banana, peeled, sliced
½ cup halved strawberries
8 baby carrots

Place all ingredients in blender.
Add 1 cup crushed ice and
blender until almost smooth.
Serve immediately. Makes
2 smoothies.

Mango trees can grow to be 65 feet tall, live to be 300 years old and still bear fruit. Its taproot can grow to 20 feet below the surface.

When ripe, mangoes are soft and very juicy. The best place to eat a really ripe, really juicy mango is in a bathtub!

Coconut Cream Splash

1 cup low-fat milk or soy milk
1 (6 ounce) carton low-fat
      coconut-cream pie yogurt
1½ cups frozen mangoes
1½ cups cantaloupe pieces
1 large banana, peeled, sliced

Place all ingredients into blender
and process until smooth. Pour
into glasses or pour over ice
and serve immediately. Makes
2 smoothies.

Two antennas met on a roof, fell in
love and got married. The ceremony
wasn't much to look at, but the
reception was great!

Tangerine Lady

1 cup orange-tangerine juice,
    chilled
⅓ cup carrot juice, chilled
1 cup canned pineapple chunks
    with juice
1 banana, peeled, halved

Place all ingredients plus
pineapple juice in blender with
several ice cubes and process
until creamy. Makes 2 smoothies.

Why did the turkey cross the road?
To prove he wasn't chicken!

Fruit Medley

1 cup low-fat soy milk
½ cup silken tofu
1 cup frozen mixed berries
2 oranges, peeled, separated
1 banana, peeled, sliced
1 apple, cored, quartered

Place oranges, banana and apple in plastic wrap and freeze about 1 hour.

Place all ingredients in blender with several ice cubes and process until creamy. Makes 2 to 3 smoothies.

How does a ghost eat an apple?
By goblin it!

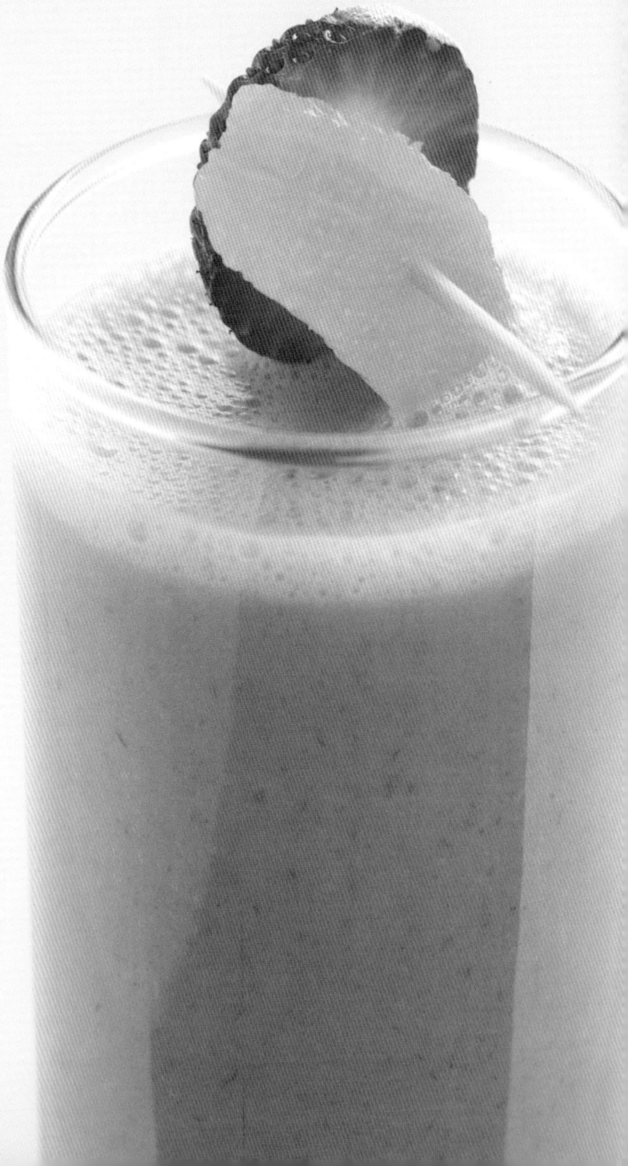

Summer Freeze

½ cup low-fat milk
½ cup orange juice
2 apples, cored, quartered
2 oranges, peeled, separated
2 kiwifruit, peeled, quartered
½ cup frozen strawberries

Place all ingredients in blender
with several ice cubes and
process until creamy. Makes
2 smoothies.

*Apples are more efficient than
caffeine at waking you up in
the morning.*

Avocado Shot

1 large avocado, peeled, pitted
2 teaspoons low-fat sweetened
   condensed milk

Place all ingredients in blender
with several ice cubes and
process until desired consistency.
Makes 1 smoothie shot.

Avocados are sometimes called
"alligator pears."

Horned fruit, Kiwano® or melano, is
an orange vegetable with points or
horns over its skin. It is mainly
ornamental, but some people eat
its green seed-filled center that is
goo-like and bitter.

Nutty Avocado Pepper-Upper

1 cup low-fat milk or soy milk
1 ripe avocado, peeled, pitted
1 cup frozen blueberries
2 tablespoons slivered almonds
½ teaspoon stevia natural
    sweetener

Place all ingredients and
several ice cubes in blender.
Process until smooth and serve
immediately. Makes 1 smoothie.

Stevia is an all-natural sweetener
that is sweeter than honey.
It has no calories or sugar.
Just ⅛ teaspoon stevia equals
1 tablespoon honey.

Get Your Daily Doses

The U.S. Department of Agriculture suggests we need to eat five to nine servings of fruits and vegetables every day.

- 1 serving of sliced fruit or vegetable = ½ cup

- 1 serving of fruit or vegetable = 1 apple or 1 pear, etc.

- 1 serving of greens (spinach, lettuce, etc.) = 1 cup

Teenage girls need 3 servings of fruit and 4 servings of vegetables.

Teenage boys need 4 servings of fruit and 5 servings of vegetables.

Active men and women need 3 servings of fruit and 4 servings of vegetables.

Small children and inactive adults need 2 servings of fruit and 3 servings of vegetables.

Veggie Smoothies

Carrot Cake Snack-A-Roo

1 cup pineapple-coconut juice
    or orange juice, chilled
1 (6 ounce) carton low-fat
    vanilla yogurt
¾ cup baby carrots
½ cup frozen pineapple chunks
1 tablespoon shredded
    sweetened coconut
1 - 2 tablespoons honey
1 whole graham cracker, optional
¼ cup sliced almonds, optional

Place all ingredients in blender
except almonds. Add about
½ cup ice cubes in blender and
process until smooth. Pour into
glass and sprinkle almonds on
top. Makes 2 smoothies.

*TIP: If you would like to have layers in
your smoothie, use two blenders to
alternate different smoothie flavors.*

*TIP: Do not give honey to babies under
1 year old.*

Carrot Topper

1 (10 ounce) can carrot juice,
    chilled
6 apricots, pitted
½ cup peeled, sliced mango
2 tablespoons honey

Place all ingredients in blender
with several ice cubes and
process until creamy. Makes
2 smoothies.

Carrots were originally round and
purple, red, white and blackish
yellow. The Dutch developed
the orange carrot to match their
national colors. The French
developed the elongated shape we
have today.

An Apple (and a Carrot) a Day

1 cup apple juice, chilled
¼ cup applesauce
8 baby carrots
1 large apple, cored, quartered
½ cup peeled, sliced cucumber

Place all ingredients in blender with several ice cubes and process until creamy. Makes 2 smoothies.

When you cut an apple in half horizontally, you'll see a star.

The "World's Longest Carrot" was 19 feet, ⅞ inches long and was recorded in 2007.

Creamy Carrot
Seeing-I Smoothie

1 (10 ounce) can carrot juice, chilled
2 (6 ounce) cartons low-fat vanilla yogurt
8 - 10 baby carrots
½ large lime, peeled

Place all ingredients in blender with several ice cubes and process until creamy. Makes 2 smoothies.

Carrots really can help you see in the dark! Vitamin A is known to prevent "night blindness," and carrots are loaded with Vitamin A (beta carotene).

The average person will consume 10,866 carrots in a lifetime.

Berry-Carrot Juicer

½ cup apple juice, chilled
½ cup low-fat milk
8 baby carrots
1 cup frozen mixed berries

Place all ingredients in blender
with 1 cup ice cubes and
process until creamy. Makes
1 smoothie.

The most digestible smoothies are
creamy because all parts of fruits
and vegetables are broken down and
are easily absorbed into the body.

Tomato-Carrot Eye-Opener

½ cup tomato juice, chilled
2 cups cored, quartered
      tomatoes or 1 (16 ounce)
      can stewed tomatoes
½ cup sliced carrots
½ cup sliced celery

Place all ingredients in blender
with 1 to 2 cups ice cubes and
process until creamy. Makes
2 smoothies.

The undisputed best ingredients for
smoothies are fruits and vegetables.
Additions such as ginseng, bee
pollen, spirulina, brewer's yeast,
wheat grass, wheat germ and whey
protein are nutritional boosters.

Red Devil

⅔ cup tomato juice, chilled
1 small tomato, quartered
¼ honeydew melon, peeled,
      chopped
1 carrot, peeled, sliced

Blend all ingredients and serve
over ice. Makes 1 smoothie.

Every year since the 1940's Valencia,
Spain has hosted a tomato-
throwing spectacle. People come
from all over the world just for
the fun of throwing more than 100
metric tons of ripe tomatoes at
each other.

Never ask a 3-year-old to hold a
tomato. Anonymous

Gazpacho in a Glass

1 (16 ounce) can tomato juice,
    chilled
½ cup vegetable stock, chilled
3 large tomatoes, quartered
1 green bell pepper, cored,
    quartered
1 small onion, peeled, quartered
½ medium cucumber, peeled, sliced
¼ cup red wine vinegar
½ teaspoon garlic powder

Puree tomatoes in blender. Add
remaining ingredients except garlic
powder and blend for about
20 seconds.

Taste mixture and season with
a little garlic powder, salt and
pepper. Taste again and adjust
seasonings, if needed.

Chill in refrigerator for about
30 minutes. Makes 3 to 4 smoothies.

Green Gorilla

2 cups fresh spinach, stemmed
1 medium, ripe avocado,
      peeled, pitted
¾ cup frozen mango slices
¾ cup frozen pineapple chunks

Pour ¾ cup water and 4 ice cubes into blender and add all ingredients. Process until smooth and serve immediately. Makes 2 smoothies.

TIP: A garnish of asparagus is always nice.

Green smoothies are great! Most of us don't get our recommended daily dose of nutrients from fruits and vegetables and green smoothies are terrific solutions. With lots of fruit, you'll never taste the vegetables.

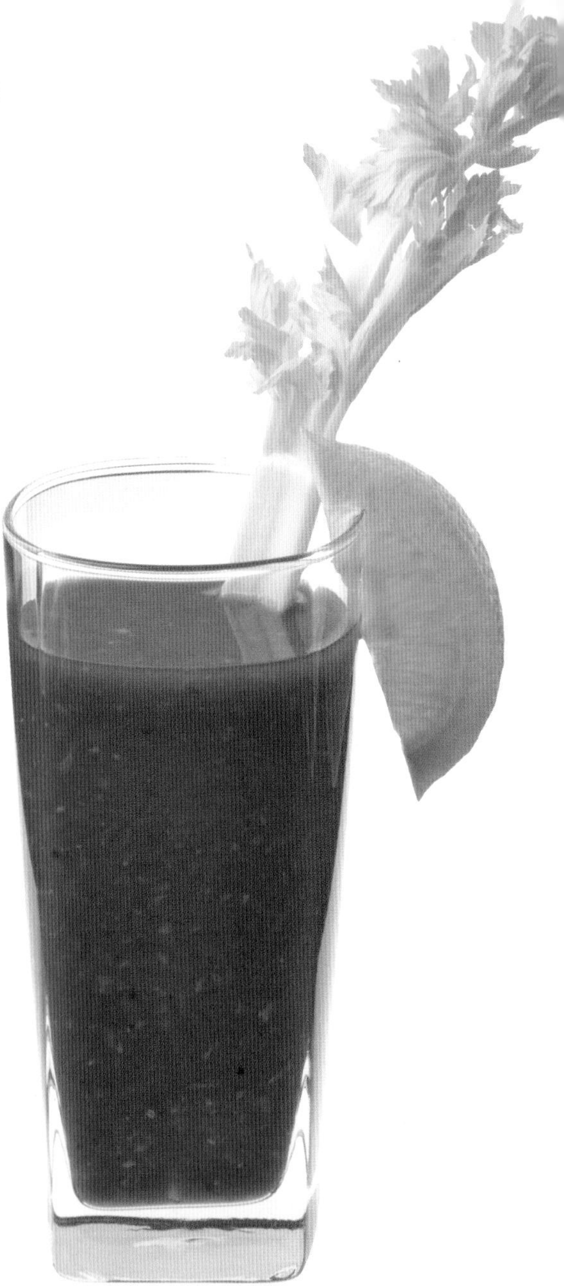

Summer Salad Smoothie

1 cup tomato juice, chilled
1 (6 ounce) carton low-fat
   vanilla yogurt
1 large tomato, quartered
1 large cucumber, peeled,
   sliced
2 ribs celery, sliced
1 tablespoon minced onion

Place all ingredients in blender
with a dash of salt and pepper
and several ice cubes and
process until creamy. Makes
2 smoothies.

*TIP: To give it a little zip, sprinkle some
cayenne pepper or Tabasco® sauce
in the blender.*

*Laughing is good exercise. It's like
jogging on the inside! Anonymous*

Popeye's Drink

½ cup apple juice, chilled
2 cups chopped baby spinach
1 cup baby carrots
1 apple, seeded, quartered

Place spinach in blender with juice and about ½ cup water. (Add more if needed.) Process into fine pieces.

Place remaining ingredients in blender with several ice cubes and process until creamy. Makes 1 to 2 smoothies.

In 2004 Popeye and spinach were given the distinction of being the only cartoon character ever recognized with green lights on the Empire State Building. The words "jeep" and "goon" were created in the Popeye cartoons.

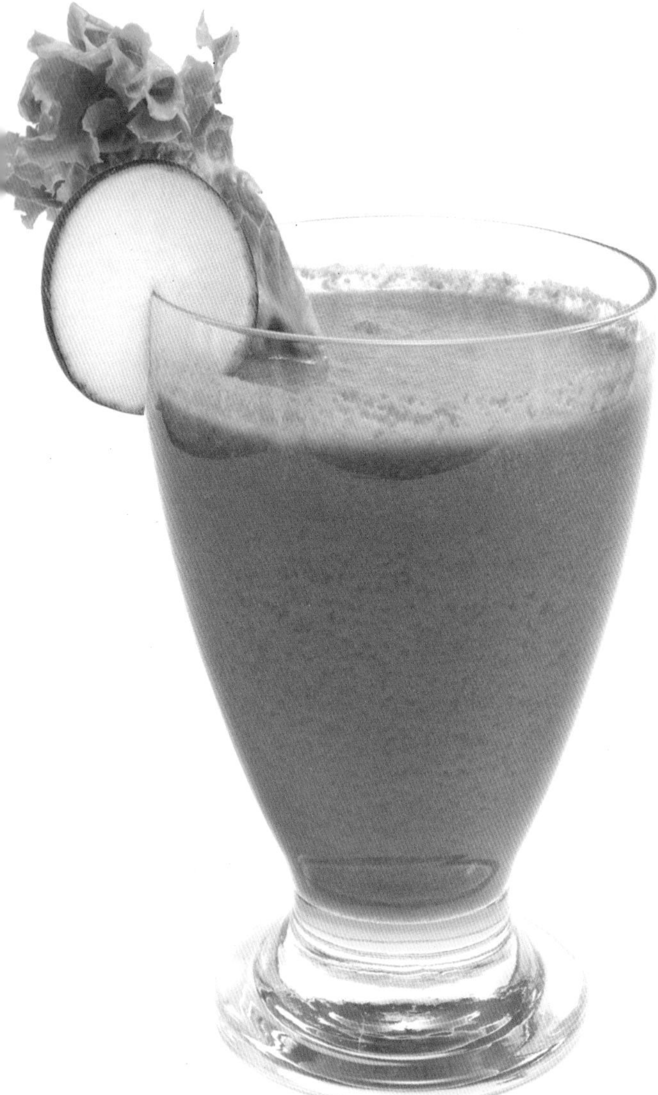

Hi-Octane Veggie Blast

Fresh, uncooked vegetables have more nutrients and minerals than those that are cooked.

1 cup fresh kale, spinach or lettuce
1 cup broccoli florets
4 - 6 baby carrots, halved
1 tomato, quartered
1 small onion, peeled, quartered
½ cup hulled sunflower seeds
¼ cup picante sauce
1 - 2 cloves garlic
1 - 2 teaspoons fresh lemon juice

Place kale in blender, add 1 cup water and pulse several times. Add remaining ingredients with several ice cubes and blend until smooth. Makes 2 smoothies.

You can't hide a piece of broccoli in a glass of milk, but no one knows when you put it in a smoothie. If you don't like the taste, add fruit. It overpowers the flavor of vegetables.

Swamp Monster

They will never guess the secret ingredient!

1 cup apple juice, chilled
1 cup kale
1 banana, peeled, sliced
1 orange, peeled, separated
1 pear, cored, sliced
1 cup honeydew melon pieces

Place kale in blender with juice
or 1 cup water and blend. Add
all fruit and blend until smooth.
Makes 2 smoothies.

*To change the color of a " green"
smoothie, use red cabbage and it
won't look so strange to you.*

St. Patrick's Day Smash

2-3 cups lightly packed
　　　cabbage leaves
1 banana, peeled, sliced
1 cup frozen unsweetened
　　　strawberries
1 teaspoon stevia or sweetener

Place 1 cup water and all
ingredients in blender with
several ice cubes and process
until desired consistency. Add
more water for thinner drink.
Makes 2 smoothies.

Being overweight is something
that just sort of snacks up on
you. ahajokes.com

Chocolate-Cabbage Powerhouse

You won't taste the cabbage, but your body will know it is getting the nutrients.

2 cups lightly packed fresh
     cabbage leaves
1 banana, peeled, sliced
5 dates, pitted
½ cup slivered almonds
2 tablespoons cocoa
1 teaspoon vanilla

Pour 1 cup water and cabbage into blender and pulse several times. Add all remaining ingredients and several ice cubes and blend until smooth. Makes 2 smoothies.

Lettuce Entertain You

2 cups butter lettuce leaves
2 oranges, peeled, separated
1 bananas, peeled, sliced

Place lettuce in blender with
about 1 cup cold water and
blend. Add fruit and blend until
desired consistency. Makes
2 smoothies.

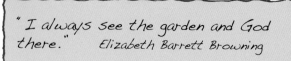

" I always see the garden and God
there."   Elizabeth Barrett Browning

Don't Tell the Kids Smoothie

1 cup orange juice, chilled
4 florets broccoli
1 cup stemmed spinach
4 - 6 baby carrots
1 orange, peeled, separated
1 apple, cored, quartered

Place all ingredients in blender with several ice cubes and process until creamy. Makes 2 smoothies.

"A wise man will make more opportunities than he finds."
Francis Bacon

Tangy Veggie Fusion

1 (16 ounce) can tomato juice,
    chilled
¼ cup fresh lemon juice
1 medium cucumber, peeled,
    quartered
½ red bell pepper, seeded,
    quartered
1 rib celery, sliced
3 green onions with tops,
    divided
2 tablespoons Worcestershire
    sauce

Place all ingredients, except
green onions, in blender and add
a dash of salt and pepper.

Add 1 green onion and several
ice cubes and process until
desired consistency. Garnish
each glass with green onion.
Makes 2 smoothies.

Seeing Red

1 cup tomato juice, chilled
1 medium cucumber, peeled,
      quartered
1 avocado, peeled, pitted
1 red bell pepper, seeded,
      quartered
1 rib celery, sliced
3 baby carrots
¼ cup fresh cilantro

Place all ingredients in blender
with several ice cubes and
process until creamy. Makes
2 smoothies.

" Never, never, never, never give up."
        Winston Churchill

Romaine Mania

1 head Romaine lettuce leaves
2 oranges, peeled, separated
1 bananas, peeled, sliced
½ cucumber, sliced

Place 1 cup cold water in blender with all ingredients and process until creamy. Makes 2 smoothies.

If all the strawberries produced in California in one year were placed end to end, they would circle the world 15 times. hungrymonster.com

166

Cucumber Cocktail

1 cup apple juice, chilled
2 large cucumbers, peeled, sliced
1 large apple, cored, seeded,
    quartered

Place all ingredients in blender
with several ice cubes and
process until creamy. Makes
1 smoothie.

*TIP: For a thinner smoothie, add more
    apple juice or water.*

*The difference between apple juice and
apple cider is juice is pasteurized and
cider is not.*

*Why did Eve want to move to New
York City?*

She fell for the Big Apple!

*It is better to find a whole worm in
an apple than half a worm.*

Index

A

B

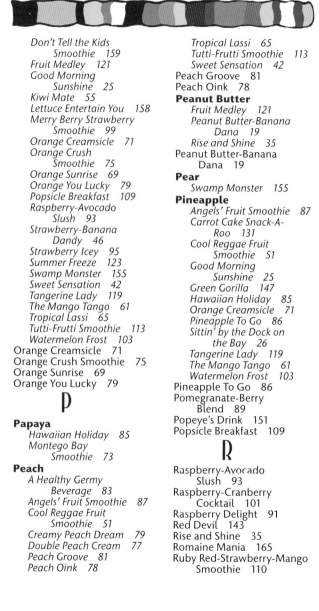

W

Watermelon
Summertime Watermelon
    Smoothie   105
Watermelon Frost   103
Watermelon Frost   103
Wheat Germ
A Healthy Germy
    Beverage   83
Berry Blessing   31
Sweet and Dandy   37
Whey Cool   97

Y

Yogurt
A Healthy Germy
    Beverage   83
Angels' Fruit Smoothie   87
Berry Blessing   31
Berry Mix-Up   29
By Golly, Wow!   39

Cookbooks Published by Cookbook Resources, LLC
Bringing Family and Friends to the Table

**cookbook
resources** LLC
www.cookbookresources.com
Your Ultimate Source for Easy Cookbooks